Gilding

The Five Mile Press

The Five Mile Press Pty Ltd
22 Summit Road
Noble Park Victoria 3174

First published 1996
Text copyright © Elisabeth Garratt
Design and production: Emma Borghesi
Editor: Maggie Pinkney
Photography and styling: Neil Lorimer
Illustrations: Joy Antonie

Printed in Hong Kong by South China Printing (1988) Co.

National Library of Australia Cataloguing-in-Publication data

Garratt, Elisabeth.
Gilding with Dutch gold leaf.

ISBN 0 86788 503 3
ISBN 0 86788 501 7 (pbk)

1. Gilding. 2. Gold-leaf. 3. Gilding - Technique - History. I. Title.
745.75

Gilding

Dutch Gold Leaf • Techniques and Projects

by Elisabeth Garratt

The Five Mile Press

To my children

Julian and Laura

Contents

Introduction

'Gold.' The very utterance of the word evokes an image of wealth and opulence. With its distinctively rich, regal glow gold is one of the most coveted metals on earth. The art of gilding, the process of covering an object with a thin layer of gold to achieve the effect of solid gold, is as old as recorded history. The techniques involved, however, have been a closely guarded secret, being passed down through the centuries from father to son and master gilder to apprentice. Even today, professional gilders are extremely reticent about the finer details of their exacting art.

My aim is to demystify the gilding process and to open the doors of this lavish art to the home renovator and craftsperson. At this point I must emphasize that I have used Dutch gold leaf on all the projects in this book. Dutch gold leaf is an imitation gold leaf which is a composite of copper and zinc, and is sometimes also known as Dutch metal or shlagmetal. I believe this most functional yet attractive leaf has been unfairly neglected in other books on gilding. It effectively simulates the rich, mellow hue of pure gold leaf and gives a glorious lustre unobtainable with gold paint. Moreover, once a coat of shellac has been applied it will not tarnish.

Dutch gold leaf has several major advantages that render it accessible to the modern craftsperson. For example, it is far less expensive than pure gold leaf, and may be applied quickly and with ease, without the need for costly specialist tools. This is not to say that gilding with pure gold leaf is beyond the scope of the average person, but it certainly requires a far greater degree of expertise and financial commitment. Also, it would not be prudent to apply real gold leaf to mass-produced objects, whereas Dutch gold leaf can be used to transform a wide range of pieces — from large carved mirror frames to small objects made of wood, plaster, terracotta, papier mâché, most metals or even plastic. By following the simple step-by-step directions in the following pages you can add a subtle, sumptuous glow of gold to your house without a huge financial outlay.

All the materials used in the projects in this book are available from specialist craft shops. Alternatively, if you write to me, care of my postal address on page 73, I can arrange to send my gilding kits to you anywhere in Australia or New Zealand.

I hope you will find this book a practical and helpful guide to enriching your home with the splendour of gold.

To all of you who fall under the spell of gold and choose gilding as your art, the Midas touch is yours — the ability to turn your world to gold.

Elisabeth Garratt

Elisabeth Garratt
MELBOURNE, 1996

A History of Gilding

*G*old has been prized throughout the centuries, not only
for its beauty but also for its very special properties.
As well as being one of the most durable of metals, in that
it does not corrode or break down with air or water, it is
also amazingly pliable. It can be moulded, beaten, melted
and even poured. Its malleability and durability are dem-
onstrated by the fact that a cubic centimetre of solid gold
can, amazingly, be beaten out to the size of a tennis court.

This gilded and painted Egyptian mummy dates from 320 BC–30 BC.

Archaeological records show that from ancient times small pieces of pure gold were beaten between animal hides to form very fine gold leaf. This leaf was then glued onto readily-available and less expensive materials such as wood, bronze, copper or silver to achieve the appearance of solid gold at a fraction of the cost. This process, known as gilding, has been shrouded in secrecy throughout its long history, and consequently techniques have hardly changed over the centuries.

Sumptuous and highly-prized, gold has been used through the ages to show reverence for the afterlife or to promote respect and even adulation for emperors and kings. The Egyptian civilisation was one of the first to apply gold as a decorative medium. Examples of gilded funerary objects date back as far as 500 BC, yet the exact period in which gilding began is difficult to ascertain. This is due to the fact that there was a scarcity of precious metals in the years following ancient Egyptian times, and so tombs were pillaged and many ancient artifacts were stolen and sold, or melted down and re-used. It is this ancient recycling of materials that distorts the authenticity of dating measures and makes it difficult to say exactly when gilding began.

When gold was still plentiful it was used extensively by Egyptian royalty to decorate furniture, vases, bowls and other objects. These artifacts were placed in the tombs of the deceased to accompany them into the afterlife, according to their beliefs. The Egyptians decorated and enriched tombs, coffins and mummified bodies with gold leaf — often the faces, hands, toes and even genitals of the embalmed bodies would be gilded.

The reason for this extravagant practice was to show that the deceased was royal or at least of exceptional wealth and so could be distinguished from the common people in the afterlife. Daily scenes were often carved or etched into the coffins and these too were picked out with gold leaf. This was to further demonstrate the status of the deceased, and to ensure they would receive due respect in the life to follow.

The Egyptians were not the only civilisation to invest gold with a symbolic, holy value. The ancient Greeks and later the Romans also used the gilding process to embellish their tombs, palaces and places of worship. These were usually made of heavy stone and marble, and inscriptions carved into them were often highlighted with gold leaf. These methods are still used today on tombstones, directory tablets and statuary.

The Egyptian custom of producing gilded coffin portraits directly influenced the art of the Byzantine Empire, culminating in the production of icons. This sumptuous art form, so typical of the distinctive Byzantine style, made lavish use of gilding. The subject, usually a holy figure, was depicted in brilliantly coloured robes — often rich blood-reds and regal blues — offset by a gilded halo. The gold of the halo imparted an ethereal effect, suggesting the divine glory of God. A similar style was later adopted by the Russian Orthodox and Catholic churches to depict God, Jesus, the Virgin Mary and saintly figures, and has survived with little modification to the present day.

During the Middle Ages, most artistic and decorative pursuits were confined to holy or religious purposes. From the seclusion of monasteries, monks used the gilding process to embellish holy statuary and depictions of significant events. Reliquaries were commonly resplendent with gold leaf as were many instruments of liturgy, such as processional crosses, chalices, holy shrines and altars. However, perhaps one of the most significant uses of gilding in the Middle Ages was associated with sacred books and the preservation of holy manuscripts. Monks and scribes were bound by holy vows to painstakingly transcribe these sacred scriptures and histories. Initial capital letters were often enlarged and profusely adorned and enriched with gold leaf as were the decorative borders on each page. These pages were made of vellum, a fine animal skin, and were kept between stiff wooden boards. The reverence and care taken with the production and storage of these books is the reason that so many have survived to the present.

By the late fourteenth century the rigid, static society of the Middle Ages had begun to break down under the influence of new ideas and attitudes. While the church continued to play an important role it lost its total domination over the people, and a new emphasis on the role of the individual began to emerge. This new freedom of thought ultimately led to the flowering of all the arts in the period known as the Renaissance. Beginning in Florence at the start of the fifteenth century, this movement spread through the Italian peninsula before sweeping across Europe, with each country developing its own interpretation of the style.

St John the Evangelist, *c. 1475–80 (detail). This French illumination on vellum is from the Wharncliffe Hours. It is the work of Maitre Francois.*

Opposite:
The Crucifixion, *c. 1349, by Paolo*
Veneziano. Here gold leaf has been
used to magnificent effect.

Homes during this period were sparsely furnished, yet the pieces commissioned were exceedingly large and monumental. Of particular popularity in Italy during this time were the 'cassoni'. These were huge chests, similar in function to our 'hope chests', which were used to store the family linen and clothes. These cassoni were sometimes reminiscent in shape of sarcophagi and were richly carved and profusely decorated with gilding. With the loosening of the Church's once supreme rule, the subject matter of such carvings began to deviate from religious themes to the depiction of the triumphs of the Roman generals or other events from early Roman history which were a source of pride.

This shift in outlook was also reflected in the architecture of the period. Renaissance architects turned away from the gothic style of the late Middle Ages and instead drew inspiration from the buildings of the ancient Greeks and Romans. They embraced such classical forms as the dome, the tunnel vault, the round arch and the use of columns. Gilding continued to be used to adorn churches, religious paintings, and the frames surrounding them.

The classicism of the Renaissance period gradually gave way to the exaggerated, overdecorated styles of baroque architecture. This dramatic, even bizarre, departure from all preceding styles began in Rome in the late sixteenth century and spread throughout Italy and other parts of Europe. This movement was basically a revolt against the freshness and purity of classicism.

The baroque period heralded a significant change in the construction of palaces, which were now built on an expanded, monumental scale. In turn, the gilding process changed. Detail was sacrificed in order to cover the vast size of these structures. The overall effect became more important than the intricate details of previous periods. Gilding was used extensively during this era, and blended richly with the vivid and luxurious fabrics and the contrasting surface textures.

Gesso, a white, chalky substance, was also widely used both as a base for gilding or left exposed. Often a form was built up by applying successive layers of gesso which was useful in carving the lavish ornamentation so typical of this time. Shellfish, ear-shaped carvings and grotesque sea-creatures were popular decorations for the often-theatrical and florid furniture of this period.

Masterpieces by such great contemporary painters as Rembrandt and Rubens were displayed in lavishly decorated gilded frames. These were individually carved and meticulously water-gilded by experienced craftsmen, the wood having been seasoned for years beforehand. The time and expertise that went into such frames was reflected in their price. Only the very wealthy could afford them.

The ornate, decadent style of baroque decoration was used extensively by royalty throughout the palaces of Europe. However, no king or queen in history ever made such extravagant use of gilding as did France's Sun King, Louis XIV. Where gold leaf had previously been used to glorify God and the afterlife, he used it to elevate himself to godlike proportions. In those days, a monarch's power was judged by the size and grandeur of his court, so Louis XIV set about building the largest and most splendid palace in Europe — Versailles. In this he succeeded, although he did not live to see it completed, and its incredible extravagance helped to sow the seeds of the French Revolution at the end of the following century.

Louis XIV became a great patron of the arts, and gathered together some of the finest artists and craftsmen in Europe to produce furnishings worthy of his magnificent and extensively gilded palace. His special workshop, the Gobelin factory, produced luxurious furniture, tapestries and other decorative objects for Versailles and later for the palaces and public buildings of Europe. By now, France had become the fashion centre of the Western world.

In the early eighteenth century the aristocracy and an upwardly-mobile middle class began to dominate the social background of the arts. Townhouses and homes in the country were renovated to be conducive to informal entertaining and frivolous conversation. The mood at this time was feminine, light and charming, and several new pieces of furniture were created to reflect this feeling.

Many richly gilded and upholstered settees were produced with elegantly carved little tables, but the most popular item of furniture of the period was the bombé commode. This was virtually a chest of drawers, on finely-carved cabriole legs, that had an almost 'swollen' appearance in the centre. Commodes were usually made from lightly-coloured woods and were intricately decorated with marquetry. Such pieces were given further embellishment by the addition of chiselled ormolu mounts and handles. These gilt adornments had the practical purpose of protecting the wood beneath. Bombé commodes were exceedingly prestigious pieces of furniture which stood at waist height and were usually set beneath an ornately-framed painting or mirror.

Gilt chairs, which were also an extremely popular fashion item of the time, came to be acquired the world over once this frivolous new style had firmly taken hold. Known as the rococo style, it was the final phase of the baroque period.

Developing in France in the early eighteenth century, this decadent style soon spread to other European countries. Rococo buildings lacked the monumentality of baroque construction, being finer and lighter. However, rococo style was even more ornate than baroque, and made even more use of gold leaf. Whereas baroque interiors were typically decorated in deep purples and burgundies, rococo architects favoured pale blue, oyster and cream, offset by swirls of gilded wall decorations.

Oriental furniture influenced rococo decor, and a Chinese-inspired style known as chinoiserie became popular at this time. Many European courts had a 'Chinese room' featuring extensive lacquering and gilding. Such rooms, resplendent with the exotic flavours of the East, were often set aside for the king's mistresses.

The Chinese and Japanese had themselves been using gold leaf for many centuries. From early times the Chinese had adorned wood, pottery and textiles with beautiful designs in gold. Gilding was also used for religious purposes — many of the statues of Buddha are gilded.

The Japanese had developed a method of decoration called 'chinkin bori', which involved carving patterns into Japanese lacquerwork and using gold inlay in the design. They also trailed coatings of gesso with a stick over an otherwise plain surface to make interesting designs and shapes which were later gilded. However, Japanese art and gilding techniques did not reach Europe until the last decades of the nineteenth century, following the opening up of Japan to the West.

By the late 1750s neoclassicism had largely replaced rococo style. This return to the straight lines, harmonious proportions and sense of order of the ancient world was inspired by the excavation of the ancient cities of Pompeii and Herculaneum. Neoclassical buildings often incorporated colonnades of Ionic pillars, classical-style cornices and draped statues, the overall effect being stately, solid and imposing. Architectural details and statuary were often highlighted with gold leaf. The wealthy classes of America, anxious to keep up with European fashions, adopted this style which they called the Federal style. Neoclassical-style furniture, also known as Louis XVI style, was plainer and straighter than its rococo counterpart.

After the French Revolution, Napoleon wanted to surround himself with objects which were elegant and suited to the leader of a great military empire. The result was the straight, heavy, Roman-inspired furniture of the early nineteenth century, known as Empire style.

Gilding was used a great deal on most of the flamboyant furniture of this period, either by itself or as an embellishment for beautifully polished dark woods like mahogany and ebony. Black and gold furniture was very much in vogue as were mirrors which were intended to make rooms seem larger. These mirrors were sometimes circular and convex or oblong-shaped with heavily gilded frames, which were often topped by large gilded birds and dragons.

Most Empire-style motifs paid tribute to Napoleon's power. For example, laurel wreaths, symbolising victory, were popular, as were sheaves of wheat, bees and cornucopia, all of which represented prosperity. Napoleon's conquest of Egypt in 1798 was proudly commemorated by the abundant use of Egyptian motifs such as sphinxes and lions' heads on much of the furniture of the time.

During the same period, the predominant fashion in England was known as Regency style after the Prince Regent. Most Regency-style furniture combined Egyptian, Chinese and gothic motifs with neoclassical elements. Sofas with scrolls at each end were typical of this period, as were elegant sideboards and overmantel mirrors. The furniture was similar to that of the Empire period, although perhaps a little less flamboyant.

Guilds, which had been set up between 1100 and 1400 to ensure the high standards of craftsmen's work, were virtually dismantled prior to Napoleon's rise to power. This led to an increase in illegal and often fraudulent practices as craftsmen were left free to compete on a commercial basis, supplying goods for a wider but far less discerning clientele than in previous centuries. With the decline in the patronage of royalty and the wealthy upper classes, standards of

Leatherbound books embellished with gold leaf.

craftsmanship considerably declined. Goods were now being made to meet prices rather than standards.

A growing merchant class began to emulate the aristocracy, and was soon acquiring gilded objects that were once beyond the reach of any but the richest classes. The merchant class was aided in this by advances in mechanisation that meant objects could be produced quickly, and thus for far less exorbitant rates. For example, gilded picture frames were now being mass-produced. This process involved lengths of moulded wood being passed through a machine which glued on a thick foil that looked like gold leaf. These lengths were then assembled into frames. Base metal foils, glazes and other mediums that simulated gold leaf were also in demand during this period, as people were keen to achieve an opulent effect at a fraction of the cost of pure gold leaf.

Gilding continued to feature periodically in the ensuing years, particularly during the High Victorian era, with its ornamental excesses, and into the 1920s and '30s when the Art Deco style was in vogue. This movement made extensive use of silver leaf and was innovative in the use of gold leaf.

Gilding is still used in many specialist fields today. Calligraphers, for example, use gold leaf in a similar fashion to that of the ancient scribes who copied out and embellished holy scriptures. Initial capitals are often profusely decorated with gold leaf to offset the rest of the beautifully formed lettering.

Gold leaf is also used by bookbinders to decorate the spines of leatherbound volumes, and is rolled onto the borders of leather desktops to add interest to embossed designs.

Gilding is also widely used by signwriters — many shop windows are emblazoned with pure gold lettering. Similarly, gold leaf lettering is used on the sides of trucks, cars and boats. Gilding is an intrinsic part of the work of monumental stonemasons, and also plays an extensive role in the work of conservators, curators and restoration experts. Most galleries and antique specialists call on such services to keep their precious artifacts in pristine condition.

Finally, the art of gilding is kept alive by the hobbyist who wants to create beautiful objects, and the keen home renovator who wishes to restore an old house to its former glory.

The Basic Method

As long as you follow the simple steps outlined in this chapter you should find gilding with Dutch gold leaf fairly straightforward. However, it would be advisable to try this method out on a test piece first rather than beginning on an object you treasure.

I strongly advise you to have any antique pieces valued before gilding them with Dutch gold leaf. In some cases you may be advised that your heirloom would be more valuable in its present condition, or that it warrants gilding with pure gold leaf by an experienced professional.

Pure Gold Leaf

There are basically two techniques of applying pure gold leaf: water-gilding and oil-gilding. Water-gilding is more exacting and time-consuming than oil-gilding, and requires special tools. However, it yields magnificent results — it is only through water-gilding that gold leaf can be burnished (or polished) to a state of brilliance.

One of the problems of gilding with pure gold leaf — apart from the prohibitive cost — is that it is so fine that it is virtually transparent, requiring three sheets, one on top of the other, to achieve a solid effect. Dutch gold leaf, on the other hand, needs only one sheet to cover its area — being twenty-five times heavier than pure gold leaf. This makes it easier to handle and, of course, much quicker to apply.

Materials Suitable for Gilding

The following materials lend themselves to being gilded with Dutch gold leaf: raw wood, plaster, cement, paper, cardboard, papier mâché, bisque-fired clays, terracotta, resin, most metals and plastics. If you want to use Dutch gold leaf on fired clays or porcelain objects you'll first of all need to apply a special preparation substance such as Easy Surface Preparation (ESP). This contains penetrol which provides a 'key' that enables the successive layers to adhere to glossy surfaces.

Materials

- Dutch gold leaf
- Shellac (ready-mixed or flakes)
- Methylated spirit
- Water-based gilding size
- Gilding primer (spray or paint) or gesso and a water-based flat paint (rusty red)
- White cotton gloves (available at most chemists)
- Suitable filler
- Fine sandpaper

- Fine steelwool
- Assorted brushes
- Jars and lids
- Antiquing finish (optional)
- Gauze or velvet (optional)

Method

1 Preparing the surface

If you are gilding wood or a blemished object, fill any pits, holes or imperfections that you don't want to appear on the finished product. (Bear in mind that gold is reflective and that imperfections will not disappear under the successive layers to be applied.)

Having done this, rub down the surface with fine steelwool or sandpaper. None of the above is necessary on terracotta, craftwood, papier mâché, or similar surfaces. Make sure the surface to be gilded is sound, clean and free of dust and any steelwool shards. A tack cloth would be useful, if you have one. Otherwise simply rub down with a slightly damp, clean cloth.

2 Applying the gilding primer

The surface must be adequately primed before you start to gild. Special gilding primers are available, and these are best because they usually contain red oxide. (This effectively simulates the red bole used in traditional gilding.) Such primers are available in either paint or spray form. If using the paint-on version you may have to lightly sand the object afterwards with a fine sandpaper to remove any brushstrokes. The spray method should not require sanding although you must be careful to apply a fine, even coat and not to hold the nozzle too close, as this can produce ugly drips — which may necessitate sanding after all. If you are unable to obtain a special gilding primer I suggest that you begin with a few coats of gesso and then add a coat of water-based paint containing red oxide.

If the object has been painted with a gloss finish or an oil-based paint you'll have to strip it with paint-stripper before starting to prime. Whilst you don't have to completely remove the painted surface you need to make the glossy top layer more porous. However, if the object has been painted with a water-based paint, you

Applying the primer.

First coat of shellac.

can prime straight over it. The best test for determining whether the finish will adhere is to apply a small portion of gilding primer and leave it to dry for a few hours. If it does not scratch off easily you can proceed to apply the primer. However, if you can easily remove the primer with your fingernail then apply a coat of ESP, following the directions on the tin, before applying the gilding primer or gesso.

If using the primer on a relatively porous surface there is no need to wait until it is completely dry. The object may be gilded over as long as it is dry to the touch.

3 The first coat of shellac

Shellac is a resin used for making French polish, and provides an excellent coating for Dutch gold leaf. It seals the primer surface and prevents it from absorbing the 'size' coat (step 4.) This is most important, otherwise the size will dry rather patchily, preventing the Dutch gold leaf from adhering in some places. Shellac is available in flakes or ready-mixed in a liquid form.

If you are using flakes crush them by hand and put them in a glass jar. Then fill the jar with methylated spirit to just cover the flakes and allow them to soak. It usually takes about half an hour for them to completely dissolve. Once dissolved, stir briskly and strain through a metal strainer, an old stocking or some muslin. I prefer to use an old stocking as it can later be discarded. The shellac will clog the metal strainer which can only be re-used if it is burned off with a naked flame. (This procedure should be done outdoors, and with extreme care.)

Once the solution has been strained, use a small varnish brush to apply a coat of shellac to the primed object. (Ready-mixed shellac can of course be applied straight from the bottle.) Be wary of any drips or build-up of shellac as these may be visible under the leaf. If this situation has occurred, however, just firmly brush on some pure methylated spirit until the excess shellac has dissolved. Allow to dry.

It's a good idea to keep a small jar of methylated spirit handy and to place your brush in it at this stage. This will dissolve the shellac, so that your brush will be ready for the second coat of shellac (step 8).

4 Applying the size

'Size' is the substance that attaches the gold leaf and virtually glues it on. For this form of gilding a water-based, pressure-sensitive adhesive is used. This is usually white, and about the same consistency as PVA glue, although the latter cannot be used as a substitute. When the shellac is completely dry put a little gilding size into a small container, e.g., the lid of a jar. Using a fine good-quality brush, apply an even coat of size over the shellacked surface.

The way you apply the size is most important as it will affect the end result. The brush should not be loaded too heavily and the size should not be allowed to collect in any hollows. If you are applying size to a heavily embossed surface with many ridges and indentations it is best to 'stab' it on rather than brush it, otherwise it will collect in pools that won't dry out enough to accept the leaf. The whole object must receive a thin, even coat that is uniformly 'greyish' in colour, i.e., there should not be any really whitish sections.

It is best to apply the size thinly, then to move straight on to another section. If you continue brushing the same area over and over, in an attempt to smooth it, the size will quickly go tacky. In other words, constant brushing will do more harm than good. You'll know that the size is ready to accept the Dutch gold leaf when the entire surface has gone completely clear and there is no size visible. This usually takes about 15 minutes.

Promptly wash the brush in warm, soapy water after use to prevent the bristles from hardening and glueing together.

Note: If you try to gild before the size has gone completely clear the leaf will stick to your gloves rather than the object and will give an unsatisfactory result. You don't have to rush to lay the leaf the minute the object has gone completely clear. The surface will remain tacky for quite a few hours. If leaving it for a lengthy period it will best accept the leaf if it is protected from dust.

5 Laying the leaf

Never touch the leaf with your bare fingers. The oil in your skin can leave an unsightly fingerprint that may oxidise a few days later and be impossible to remove.

Applying the size.

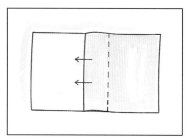

Top: *Lifting the leaf.*
Middle: *Laying the leaf.*
Lower: *Always rub away from the the join.*

Use white cotton gloves and a soft clean brush (or gauze or velvet).

First put on your white cotton gloves. If you are using a book of twenty-five leaves of Dutch gold leaf there will be a sheet of rouge paper between each leaf. To lift the leaf position one gloved hand so that the little finger is resting lightly on the leaf and blow the leaf up onto your other gloved hand to pick it up. If using the leaf which has not been interleaved with rouge paper (this is the way it is packaged in larger quantities) you'll have to find the edge of the top leaf. Because the leaves are placed one over the other they are laid in a staggered fashion, one about 3 cm to the left and the next about 3 cm to the right. This makes it easier to separate them. To do this place one gloved hand on the sheet to be lifted whilst simultaneously holding down the sheet beneath with the other gloved hand. Now gently blow the upper sheet to remove it from the rest.

Carefully place the Dutch gold leaf onto the sized object by touching it on, aiming to get the maximum amount of coverage per sheet. Let the leaf gently fall onto the object and it will stick at the slightest contact.

Depending on personal taste and the piece you are gilding, you must decide at this stage whether or not you want to achieve a crackled, antique look with a lot of the red-coloured primer showing through under the leaf. (This type of finish will occur naturally on objects with a lot of indentations, as the leaf will adhere to the uppermost areas and must be worked on to adhere to the low relief areas, grooves and indentations.)

If you want a uniform solid gold look, with little red showing through, place the whole leaves on the object, with the squares slightly overlapping one another — taking care where you place the joins as these will be visible. When rubbing the excess leaf from the object always rub away from the join rather than into it, against the grain of the leaf. There is no right or wrong side to the leaf. Don't worry if it seems to tangle or crease, as this results in that 'gilded' look, and will be hardly noticeable after the next few steps.

If working on a relatively small flat surface (e.g. a box) I prefer to tear the leaves up and place them haphazardly all over the object. This gives a more interesting look which is rich in character. If you place a whole leaf directly onto such an object you end up with an unsightly straight line that will be impossible to remove. The end result will depend on how many of the reddish areas are covered by leaf, and how many are left exposed. There are no set rules about this — the amount of uncovered area a gilder leaves visible is purely a matter of personal taste.

Use a brush to get into any areas which are hard to reach, being careful not to touch the sized areas with your gloves or brush, or the leaf will stick to them and will disturb the tackiness of the sized object. If any of the sheets of leaf have considerably overlapped, gently attempt to tear off the excess. This can then be re-used in an area that is still exposed.

It may seem as if the gold is simply not sticking and the whole object looks like a 'shaggy' mess. Don't lose heart. Any pieces that don't readily adhere are best rubbed off. These and other pieces that fall off may be re-used in any patchy spots. Areas that refuse to accept the leaf may be 'touched up', once all the leaf has been applied, by adding a very small amount of size. Again allow this to go clear, and be careful not to touch the size on any of the gold surrounding the patch.

Once the object has been covered with the leaf give it a firm rub-down with your gloved hand. There is no need to be afraid to apply a fair amount of pressure at this stage, as this should not damage the leafed surface. Run a gloved fingernail around any straight grooves to 'cut in' and give a clean edge. Polish firmly using the gloves.

6 'Distressing' the object

This step is optional and is best done on an inconspicuous area first. Using a fine steelwool, rub gently in a circular fashion over any of the raised areas — taking care not to remove any of the gilt. The idea is to darken the areas that would naturally become worn over time, thus giving the piece a rich, mellow, aged look. If you are unsure about which areas to 'distress' run your gloved hand downwards over the object. The parts which protrude and come into obvious contact are the ones which would become worn over time. Distressing looks best on objects with a lot of detail. If doing a flat-sided object, like a picture frame or box, it is best to

Four different antiquing finishes
(see page 27).

Drying the shellac.

apply this technique only to the corners and any sharp edges. Never distress the middle of a flat object as it leaves unsightly circular marks. Don't worry if the distressing doesn't show up much at this stage. You can only see the real effect of your efforts after the next step.

When you have finished distressing the object dust it off, completely removing any steelwool shards and loose bits of gilt. Cotton buds and a vacuum cleaner are often handy for this purpose.

7 The second coat of shellac

Still wearing the cotton gloves, carefully move the object to a clean area, and cover this working surface with plain white paper, e.g. butchers' paper. Don't use newspaper as you could end up with newsprint stuck to the bottom of the gilded object.

Take your container of shellac and shellac brush and apply a light, even coat, methodically doing one section at a time. Remember not to brush over the same area twice. Any drips and unsightly dark patches can be removed by brushing the dark area over with plain methylated spirit. This will dissolve the shellac. Bear in mind that each application of shellac will darken the object. If you apply more than two coats the piece will turn a brownish-orange colour, and it won't look gold at all.

After each section has been coated give the area a blow with a warm hairdryer or place it next to a heater. Depending on the humidity and temperature of the room in which you are working, the object can some-times 'bloom'. Blooming is when the final coat of shellac goes a dull white, milky colour, which will ruin the otherwise lustrous look of your work. It is therefore important to keep a source of heat handy and as soon as you see any 'milkiness' occur immediately apply the heat. The milkiness will disappear instantly. If heat is not applied and the object is left to dry in this state the dullness will remain.

Put your brush back into the methylated spirit jar to loosen the shellac from it. If you don't intend to use shellac again for a while, wash the brush out with warm soapy water. Leave to dry with the bristles upwards.

8 Antiquing finish

There are many antiquing finishes available. With Dutch gold leaf gilding you must always use a water-based antiquing medium — never use any oil-based products with this leaf. Antiquing finishes come in different colours. Whilst I am not particularly partial to brown as a decorator colour I find it is the best shade to use on traditional and classically-styled gilded objects. It imparts a rich, aged hue to the piece whilst not perceptibly changing the colour. Black can also be used on such pieces. White looks best on items and objects with a seaside theme, and is also the most effective colour for furniture, giving it a limed look. The colour used should reflect the style of the piece itself and also the room and setting where you wish to display it. Getting the right shade involves experimentation — and the antiquing finishes I produce lend themselves to this as they can be washed off (if done so immediately) if not to your taste.

The purpose of the antiquing finish is to tint the grooves and give the piece more depth. Once you have decided on the colour, apply it with a brush to the depths and hollows, doing small areas at a time. These areas are then blended and blotted by a sponge or rag to 'open' them up and show the gold through. If you want a heavier application you can paint the entire object with the antiquing finish and then remove it from the high spots. To obtain the exact look you want to achieve can take quite a bit of patience and experimentation.

When you are satisfied check that the finish has been evenly applied, making sure that there are no particularly dark patches. The best way to check the finish is to place the object in the position in which it will sit permanently, and then stand back some distance from it. If there are any dark spots they must be removed before the antiquing finish is thoroughly dry or it will be impossible to get rid of them without taking a fair amount of the gilt with it. You will have more control over the look of the piece if you darken it gradually, slowly building the colour up.

Your piece is now complete. You can apply another coat of shellac over the antiquing finish if you wish but you must take extreme care not to over-darken the object. A light spray of fixative or clear varnish may also be used although this is not necessary unless the object is going to receive considerable wear and tear.

Applying the antiquing finish.

Opposite: Some interesting effects can be created with variegated leaves.

In Summary

The following is a quick reminder of the basic steps in gilding:

1 Prepare the surface. Fill in, sand or steelwool to a perfect finish — if necessary.
2 Primer. This may be sprayed or painted, depending on the project.
3 Shellac. This seals the primer.
4 Size. This is the mordant that attaches the leaf.
5 Laying the leaf. Gloves must be worn for this step. Smooth off with gloved hand at the end.
6 Distressing the object (optional). This is done with a fine steelwool.
7 Shellac. The final sealing coat. Apply heat to dry off.
8 Antiquing finish (optional for an aged look).

Silver or Aluminium Leaf

To gild with silver or aluminium leaf follow the basic steps (above), noting these minor variations to steps 2 and 7:

2 Applying the primer

Apply the primer as indicated above but this should be followed by an application of black or navy blue water-based paint. A few coats of gesso could be used instead of the primer. (This changing of the base colour may also be used quite effectively under Dutch gold leaf and can produce some interesting effects. Black, white, Brunswick green, and yellow-ochre water-based paint can all look quite effective under the imitation gold.)

7 The second coat of shellac

Here a bleached or 'blond' shellac should be used for the final coat, because the orange shellac normally used would make the silver a light gold colour. This is not unattractive but the piece would no longer look silver. A spray-on varnish (e.g. Incralac by Wattyl) may also be used if the bleached shellac is difficult to obtain.

Variegated, Copper or Bronze Leaf

There are many variegated leaves available. These are leaves of copper to which heat has been applied and which have undergone a chemical reaction. Some rich fiery reds and pinks or blues and greens are haphazardly blended with the copper colour and, if used tastefully, will reward you with some truly brilliant results. To use these leaves (or plain copper or bronze) follow the same steps as for gilding with Dutch gold leaf.

The Projects

*O*nce you have mastered the basic gilding technique described in detail in the previous chapter, you may like to try your hand at some decorative objects to enhance and beautify your home. Each of these projects includes the basic procedure with a few minor variations and the inclusion of some other techniques, such as fabric stiffening, a quick découpage and the use of a crackle medium.

Overmantel Mirror Frame

With the current vogue for home decoration and restoration, and the trend towards neoclassicism, one of the most avidly sought objects is the gilded overmantel mirror frame. Large mirrors impart an instant air of grandeur, as well as making the room seem larger. If the mirror is placed opposite a window it will also reflect additional light.

Buying a Frame

Many importers stock interesting carved frames from Indonesia or the Philippines, like the one pictured on page 33. These are often French-polished, but it's worth trying to find one in its raw state so you can gild it. Also suitable for gilding are large sturdy frames made of fibreglass or resin. These, like the carved imported frames, are fairly expensive but will give a beautiful result when gilded.

A cheaper alternative is a plaster mirror frame, made up of decorative plaster lengths, and available from plaster supply stores. Admittedly, these are not nearly as strong as wooden or fibreglass frames, but if carefully gilded and put into place they make a most economical substitute. Alternatively, you may decide to gild over an old mirror frame.

Old Frames

If you plan to gild over a very old mirror frame it's advisable to have it valued first. It may well be more valuable if left in its present aged state.

If you can, remove the mirror from the back of the frame. But if this isn't possible (either because the frame is really old or because it's a plaster frame which has been poured with the mirror set into it) don't worry. You can simply allow the different processes of gilding to overlap onto the glass of the mirror, then scrape it down with a sharp blade when you've finished. Retain any pieces of gilt that come away — they can be used to poke down between the frame and the mirror in places where unsightly raw edges would otherwise be reflected in the mirror.

If you're using an old mirror frame you may need to restore it before gilding. Fill in any small chips with the appropriate filler, depending on the material of the

If you can't remove the mirror from the frame, scrape down with a sharp blade after gilding.

frame. In cases where whole sections of a moulding or design have broken away it's worth casting a special mould from dental plaster or modelling clay.

This is done by pressing the modelling substance over a section of the frame that is the same as the missing piece, and taking a mould of it. Then fill this mould with plaster of Paris or some other medium. (Ask your nearest craft store for advice.) When this has dried file or sand down any imperfections so that it fits snugly into the gap and glue it into place.

If there are gaps in the mitred joins on the frame it's best to fill these, along with any other gaps, as they will not disappear during the gilding process. In fact, they may even become more obvious.

Materials

- Large mirror frame
- Gesso
- Gilding materials as on page 20

Method

1 Having filled and repaired the frame (if necessary), rub it down with a fine steelwool or sandpaper, ensuring that the surface is free of dust or steelwool shards by going over it with a damp cloth.

2 Now add a few coats of gesso. Despite the fact that gesso isn't really necessary with this method of gilding I prefer to use it on frames and furniture which will be in use for a long time — these base coats of gesso impart a more antique look to such pieces if they become chipped. It's fine to use a commercially-prepared gesso rather than going to the trouble of mixing it yourself.

3 Sand off any obvious brushstrokes, as these will show up under the leaf, and again rub down with a damp cloth.

4 Add the gilding primer or simply use a rust-coloured, water-based paint (because the frame has already been sealed by the gesso). Sand off brushstrokes and clean the surface again.

5 You are now ready to proceed with the basic gilding process — see step 3, page 22.

Upper: *The lip on the back of a mirror frame must always be gilded because it will be reflected when the mirror is in place.*

Lower: *Empire-style chair.*

Note: When working on a mirror frame it's particularly important to gild the inside 'lip' of the frame (which faces into the mirror). Be aware that this will be reflected in the mirror when in place, and will look unsightly if left in its raw state.

Empire-style Chair

The same process (including the base coats of gesso) was used to complete the gilded Empire-style chair pictured here. The chair frame was gilded before being upholstered. It was then touched up in places where the upholsterer had accidentally knocked off some of the gilt in affixing the fabric.

Decorative Boxes

These stunning boxes make wonderful gifts that can be specially decorated to suit a particular person or room. They can be used to store a myriad of things.

After being gilded inside and out, wrapping paper featuring the works of old masters was glued to the lids and then découpaged. For full details of the materials required and the method used, see page 36.

The Document Box

This project incorporates a quick technique that simulates découpage — the art of decorating an object with paper cutouts. There are many different ways of tackling a découpage project, and it is a good idea to experiment to find which one suits you best. Methods range from applying a hundred coats of varnish to just a few quick sprays of fixative. In this project I simply applied a two-part polymer coating called Envirotex, which is available at hardware stores and specialist paint shops.

Here I have used a craftwood box with an interesting lid. Its downward-sloping edges give a frame effect to the pasted-on image.

Materials

- Craftwood box (or similar)
- Gilding materials as on page 20
- Wrapping paper of your choice
- Felt (optional)
- PVA glue
- Varnish, fixative or Envirotex

Method

1   Gild the box inside and out, except for the areas that you plan to cover with paper, following the steps on page 21. (Instead of gilding the inside you may prefer to line it with wrapping paper or felt.)

2   Carefully measure and cut out the decorative paper to go on the lid (and possibly also the sides). When the gilt is dry glue on the paper.

3   Apply varnish fixative or Envirotex to the paper.

Note: I've used a single layer of wrapping paper for all these boxes but you may sometimes wish to cut out other motifs from the same sheet and superimpose them on the oblong piece of paper glued to the lid, or to adhere smaller cutouts onto a painted surface (see Gilded Keepsake Box on page 60).

Opposite: *This frame was com-*
pleted by student Yvonne Prince in
her first lesson. It is complemented
by a bowl embellished with
fabric flowers.

Stiffened Fabric Frame and Bowl

Here Dutch gold leaf is used over stiffened fabric (and other embellishments). This technique, in which the folds and drapes of the fabric are stiffened with PVA glue to hold a permanent shape, enables you to achieve a variety of rich and interesting effects. If decorating a frame it's best to choose a flat, completely featureless one which is wide enough to support the desired embellishment. And if working on a bowl you can glue the decorations to the inside, the outside or onto the wide 'lip' — if it has one.

Composition and the choice of decorative elements are most important. Try not to mix natural items with classical ones. For example, cherubs, bows, tassels, and silk roses go well together and look splendid over fabric that has been swagged or ruched. But acorns, shells gumnuts, sunflowers and other more rustic decorations would look better on a separate frame. It is best to stay with one theme.

Another point to bear in mind is that the position of the ornaments should be balanced. Attractive arrangements that look as if the decorations have been scattered haphazardly are usually the result of careful thought. It is a good idea to work out your design first, by placing the decorations on a piece of paper and moving them around until you are happy with the arrangement. Then trace round them so you have a guide for when you come to glue them onto the object. I find it is best to have a central focal point, and to work outwards from it.

On a frame this point could be in any of the positions shown below. It's best not to place two large objects in direct competition to one another unless they are virtually the same and act as a balance to each other.

Three alternative focal points.

Opposite: *An aerial view of the wide-lipped bowl seen on page 39, showing the stiffened fabric flowers.*

In the two projects shown here I have gilded wide-lipped bowls to complement the stiffened fabric mirror frames. The following method focuses on the mirror frame but can applied to bowls or other objects.

Choice of Fabric

Any fabric will do. Calico is one of the least expensive, and gives a good texture. I find it works well to combine interesting remnants with different textures.

Materials

- Fabric (30 cm strips about 1–2 m long depending on desired effect)
- Disposable rubber gloves
- PVA glue (the 500 ml bottle is ideal)
- Stronger glue, e.g. Selley's Fix'n'Go Super Glue, Welbond, Araldite, Tarzan Super Grip
- Object to be decorated (frame or bowl)
- Ornaments to glue on, e.g. cherubs, bows, tassels, fabric flowers, shells, pine cones, etc.
- Gilding materials as on page 20
- Ice-cream container or bucket

Method

1 Once you've worked out exactly where you want to place the ornamentation, put on your rubber gloves and pour a large quantity of PVA glue into the ice-cream container. It's best not to skimp on the glue because you need a lot to thoroughly soak the fabric. You can either pour about a cupful of glue into a container or bucket and dunk the fabric in it, working the glue through with the fingers, or you can pour the glue directly onto the fabric, and then work through with the fingers.

2 When the fabric has been completely covered with glue run it through your hands to squeeze out the excess, and begin arranging it on the frame. It may be draped and swagged by folding the fabric into fine little folds and pinching either end so that the ends are tight and the centre fans out.

To get a bow effect, simply tie a bow as you would a shoelace, and fan the circular sections outwards, i.e., pull out either side vertically. If the bow is collapsing under the weight of the glue, and you want it to keep its fullness, stuff some plastic bags inside the loops to retain their shape. There are several ways you can arrange the long remaining 'ties'. You can tuck them back under to form a double bow, scrunch them all the way down, lift and drape them or pull them into gathers. If you keep the fabric moist with glue by brushing more on when it begins to dry out you can experiment with any of these effects.

At all times be careful not to expose any raw, cut edges at the sides of the ties or in the loops of the bow as these will be visible on completion of your project and will look unsightly. Try to tuck them under the edges and fold them back, rather like making a hem.

3   If the fabric has been properly soaked in the PVA it should adhere adequately to the frame. If it doesn't, brush extra PVA onto the frame or fabric and press on firmly. It's wise to lift the fabric once you are satisfied with the shape you have formed and brush extra PVA under it anyway, to be quite sure that it adheres properly. Although the PVA breaks down and softens during the gilding process it doesn't soften as much as do other available fabric stiffeners.

4   Once you are happy with the shape that the fabric is formed into, and you have glued it on, add other embellishments, such as cherubs, bows, shells, etc., depending on the style your object is taking. It is best to attach these with the stronger glue.

5   Allow the object and embellishments to dry and harden. Sand off any glue remnants on any of the flat surfaces, otherwise these will be visible under the gilt.

6   Now you can begin gilding your object, following the steps on page 21.

Note: If you are decorating a mirror frame pay particular attention to any pieces of fabric that overlap onto the area where the mirror will go. Be aware that these will later be reflected by the mirror, so they must be gilded round the edges on the back.

Decorative Crackled Frame

This project is a variation on the previous one (see page 38) and combines gilded stiffened fabric and other embellishments with a crackled-finish frame. The crackled effect is achieved by applying a crackle medium between two different coloured coats of paint. This medium causes the top coat to crack and reveal the base coat which is usually of a contrasting colour.

This process gives a rich, aged effect that goes particularly well with gilding. I prefer to use a darker-coloured base coat with a lighter top coat but it's best to experiment first until you find a combination that you're happy with.

I have used stiffened fabric drops, cherubs, tassels and a resin bow on the picture frame opposite. Although all those objects are of contrasting textures they have a similar theme. The gold leaf helps to bring them all together.

Materials

- Stiffened Fabric Frame and Bowl project materials as on page 40.
- Gilding materials as on page 20.
- Flat-sided frame
- Water-based yellow-ochre folk art paint
- Wood-sealer
- Crackle medium
- Water-based cream paint

Method

1 Stiffen the fabric and adhere it and the other objects to the frame, as on page 40.

2 Now gild them, as on page 21, trying not to let the gilding process overlap onto the remainder of the frame.

3 When dry, paint the exposed parts of the frame with the yellow-ochre paint mixed with a wood-sealer.

4 After several coats add the crackle medium and apply it according to the directions on the bottle. (These vary according to the particular brand.)

5 When the crackle medium has cured for the recommended period, add the water-based cream top coat. The paint should start to crack instantly.

Crackled and Découpaged Lamp Bases

These rather ornate ceramic lamp bases have had a crackle finish applied to the main body with a paper cutout glued to the 'cameo centre'. The raised areas have been gilded.

Materials

- Two identical lamp bases (available from ceramic art stores)
- Crackle medium
- Two similar paper cutouts
- PVA glue
- Gilding materials as on page 20
- Low-tack masking tape, e.g. Scotch Magic Tape

Method

1   Spray the entire lamp base with gilding primer (even though the gold leaf is only applied to the raised areas).

2   Apply gold leaf to the protruding areas, following the steps on page 21.

3   When the gilding is dry apply the crackle medium (as per directions on the bottle) to all the remaining areas, carefully masking off the gilded areas with masking tape.

4   When the crackle medium has cured paint on the cream coat. Spray with a clear fixative when dry.

5   Stick the cutout onto the 'cameo area' with PVA glue, then coat with varnish.

6   Apply antiquing finish over the entire lamp base. I used the Cafe Noir Antiquing Finish from my own gilding kit (see page 73) on the lamps shown here.

Opposite: *The vivid colours of the glass beads combine with the gold leaf to give an opulent, almost Byzantine look.*

Jewelled 'Book'

This richly-coloured 'book' is really a little drawer in disguise. The 'jewels' are glass beads.

Materials
- Small craftwood box with sliding drawer
- Glass beads (or other 'jewels')
- Tile adhesive
- Masking tape
- Cream folk art paint
- Grey lead pencil
- Fine ruler
- Gilding materials as on page 20

Method

1 Remove the drawer and prime the side that faces out with spray-on or paint-on gilding primer. Also prime the base and sides of the box, but not the top (where the 'jewels' will go).

2 Using a flat knife, liberally coat the top surface of the box with tile adhesive to a depth of about 10 mm. If you want a textured effect gently pat the knife over the adhesive to raise it into small peaks, rather like icing a cake.

3 Embed the beads into the desired positions, and when you're satisfied with the design leave it to dry. (It's a good idea to work out the pattern first by arranging the beads on a piece of paper beside your work area.)

4 Carefully brush the paint-on gilding primer around the beads.

5 When the primer is dry add the first coat of shellac, (step 3, page 22) then proceed to gild the back and front of the box. If you accidentally gild part of the beads they can be cleaned with a blade and steelwool afterwards.

6 Paint around the sides (or 'pages') of the box with a few coats of cream paint. When dry, rule fine lines on them with a ruler and sharp lead pencil to look like pages.

7 Now for the drawer or 'spine'. Use masking tape to mask off all but four straight lines, two at each end, and add a coat of shellac. Then proceed to gild the exposed areas. This should result in good clean, straight lines.

8 Remove the masking tape and apply a few coats of shellac. These will turn the exposed primer a deep rich colour, like an old leather book.

Above: *Shell tissue box covers and picture frames are ideal for seaside holiday homes.*

Opposite: *Gilded corbels make superbly decorative bookends. They can be bought from wholesale plaster manufacturers in either plaster or concrete.*

Page 50: *Gilding transformed this vase, bought for a couple of dollars from an opportunity shop, into an elegant piece.*

Shell Tissue Box Cover

Shells can make a very attractive decorator accessory, especially in bathrooms, holiday houses or homes by the sea. Collect shells from beaches, if you can. But they don't seem to be nearly as plentiful as they were in the shell-collecting days of my childhood, so you may have to buy them from a craft shop.

When choosing shells to decorate an object remember that the shape is more important than the colour. It's a good idea to gather as many shells of the same shape and size as you can, for making patterns. A trip to the local fish shop could supply you with enough pipis, mussel shells or oyster shells to give you a good start. The same basic method can be used to make an attractive shell frame.

Materials

- Shells, starfish, coral, etc.
- Tile adhesive
- Papier mâché or craftwood tissue box cover
- Gilding materials as on page 20

Method

1   Arrange the shells in the desired pattern on all sides of the tissue box cover, leaving a small even gap between each one. When you are satisfied with the arrangement transfer it to the work surface beside you, so that you have a good idea where each piece will go, later on.

2   Using a knife, thickly and smoothly spread the tile adhesive over the tissue box cover. A thickness of about 10 mm is ideal.

3   Embed the shells into the adhesive in the desired position. If you don't have enough shells you can drag a fork through the tile adhesive or make some other pattern to give an interesting texture. Leave to dry.

You may find that the shells on the sides of the box sag under their own weight. If so, reposition them and prop up the heavier ones by strategically placing icy-pole sticks cut to the appropriate length outside the box. You must arrest the sagging until the adhesive is stiff enough to hold the desired shape.

4   You are now ready to add the gilding primer (step 2, page 21 and proceed with the basic gilding process.

The Gilded Wedding

*G*ilded table decorations and keepsakes add a magical touch to that special day — without stretching the budget. Your newly-acquired knowledge of gilding can take you a long way towards having the kind of richly splendid wedding that most brides can only dream about. Hand-gilded decorations will make your wedding reception really special, imparting an elegantly individual touch that is difficult to achieve with mass-produced objects.

Rope Napkin Rings

These easy-to-make napkin rings lift any table setting out of the ordinary. They consist of a small length of rope with a motif or stiffened fabric attached to the join in the rope. It's best to use a heavy-duty plasticised rope from a hardware store. For six napkin rings a metre length of rope should suffice.

Materials (for six rings)

- One metre of plasticised rope
- Six decorative motifs
- Craft glue
- String
- Gilding materials as on page 20

Method

1 Cut the rope into 15 cm lengths, and glue the ends of each length together, making sure there is enough glue to stop the ends from unravelling.

2 Place each ring of rope inside a drinking glass (or some other receptacle) with a circumference of about 15 cm. This will hold the ends together while they are drying.

3 For extra strength, wrap some string around the join, once the glue has dried. Add more craft glue. Leave to dry.

4 Gild over the rings and decorations separately (see page 21).

5 When dry, glue the motifs onto the rings.

Ribbon Napkin Rings

These simple but extremely pretty napkin rings are made with stiffened ribbon that is later gilded. (The stiffened fabric technique is described in detail on page 40.)   In this project I've used a ribbon with an interesting texture.

Materials

- Ribbon cut into 130 cm lengths
- Cardboard tube covered with plastic
- PVA glue
- Plastic garbage bag
- Gilding materials as on page 20

Method

1 Tie the ribbon into a bow around the cardboard tube. When you are satisfied with the length and shape of the bow, untie it, remove it from the tube and soak the ribbon in PVA glue, squeezing out the excess.

2 Stretch the soaked ribbon out onto a work surface protected by a plastic garbage bag.

3 Tie the damp ribbon onto the plastic-covered tube again and remake your bow. It will, at this stage, look rather scrawny and lifeless. Working quickly, so the glue doesn't dry out before the bow is in the desired shape, fan out the loop sections of the bow to an attractive fullness. Allow to dry.

4 Apply gilding primer (step 2, page 21) and proceed with the gilding process.

Bonbonniere

In many European countries it's the custom to give wedding guests a small keepsake in appreciation of their wedding gift. Traditionally it has five sugared almonds attached to it, hence the name 'bonbonniere'. Being of Italian descent I have received many bonbonniere over the years. Some have been attractive and useful, while others have bordered on the vulgar or ridiculous. Gilding your own bonbonniere provides your guests with an individual keepsake with which to remember your special day — one that they may treasure for many years. Virtually any smallish object can be used. Here I have attached a decorative moulding to the lid of a small oval-shaped craftwood box, and then gilded it.

Materials

- Raw papier mâché or craftwood oval box
- Decorative motif
- Strong glue
- Five sugared almonds
- Tulle
- Ribbon to tie tulle pouch to bonbonniere
- Gilding materials as on page 20

Method

1 Using strong glue, stick the motif onto the lid of the box. Make sure you remove the excess glue that oozes out from under the motif, or you will have to sandpaper it off afterwards.

2 When the glue has dried apply the gilding primer (step 2, page 21) and proceed with the gilding process.

3 Just before the wedding day place the five sugared almonds into a circle of tulle. Tie up and attach to the gilded box.

Below: *Gilded box with five sugared almonds, and ribbon napkin ring.*

Wedding Album

Buy the best-quality album you can afford — the ones with stiff pages interleaved with vellum or mylar are the longest wearing. Removable pages are ideal but not essential. And an album with a burgundy-coloured cover will give you a headstart because this is close to the shade of the gilding primer, so if some of the gilt wears off over the years it won't look unsightly.

The motif to be glued onto the front of the album should have a romantic theme. Cherubs, bows, fleurs-de-lis and garlands of flowers all make a beautiful statement. Many brides like to echo the same theme on invitations, the cake, place-cards and serviette rings, etc.

You can gild the cover on the inside as well as the outside, or you may prefer to line it with beautiful wrapping paper (with a bridal theme).

Materials

- A good-quality photograph album
- Decorative motif (resin, plastic or wood moulding)
- Strong glue
- Gilding materials as on page 20
- Wrapping paper (optional)
- Craft glue
- Varnish or fixative

Method

1 Using a strong glue, stick the decorative motif onto the front cover of the album. Remove any excess glue that oozes out from under the motif — otherwise it will have to be sanded off later on.

2 When the glue has dried protect the inside covers of the album with paper and masking tape. Remove the pages (if removable), otherwise cover them with a plastic bag.

3 Apply the gilding primer (step 2, page 21) and then proceed with the gilding process.

4 When the outside of the cover is dry either gild it on the inside or line it with attractive wrapping paper

The attractively shaped plastic urn, shown in its gilded glory opposite, and the elegant cement urn, in their raw state.

Grecian Urn

The elegant urn pictured on the back cover was bought from a garden supply store. It is made of poured concrete and consequently has many pits and air holes in it. These could have been filled but I left them as they were to give the urn a more authentic, aged look. Because the surface is so porous it readily accepts the primer so that it gilds easily. This urn would look superb on the bridal table but the cost would be too prohibitive to use on all the guests' tables. A far less costly alternative would be attractively shaped plastic urns like the one pictured here. Although these look rather cheap and nasty in their natural state, once they are gilded they give the impression of being made of heavy stone. They are available from most discount stores.

Materials

- Urn
- Gilding materials as on page 20

Method

As described on page 21, remembering not to fill in the imperfections if using the concrete urn, and you want to achieve an aged look.

Below: *Special wedding day mementoes merit their own beautiful box.*

Keepsake Box

This lovely box can be used for storing cards, letters and other mementoes of your wedding day.

Materials

- Craftwood box
- Wood sealer or gesso
- Water-based folk art paint
- Gilding materials as on page 20
- Wrapping paper cutouts
- PVA glue
- Varnish, fixative or Envirotex

Method

1 Seal the whole box inside and out with gilding primer.
2 Paint the lid and sides with folk art paint (except for the areas to be gilded). In this project I have used cream paint.
3 Gild the borders of the lid, the raised edge at the base of the box and the inside, as on page 21.
4 Cut out paper figures and glue them to the lid.
5 When the glue is dry add the varnish, fixative or Envirotex to the paper.

A Golden Christmas

*C*hristmas is a time for rich festivities and the warmth of family and dear friends. Add a luxurious touch to this season of joy with some inexpensive yet gloriously effective gilded pieces. The projects in this section will add a beautiful glow to your home during this very special time of year.

Walnut Topiary Tree

In this project I have restricted colours to burgundy, gold and green. Walnuts, with their interesting shape and texture, look most attractive when gilded, and add an extra festive touch.

Topiary trees can of course be made in any size, using any colours or ornaments — depending on your particular colour scheme or theme. While they make wonderful Christmas decorations, they can also be used to brighten up a dinner table at any time of year, or to add interest to an otherwise dull corner.

You may wish to make a pair of topiary trees. If so, it is best to do them both at the same time, otherwise it is very difficult to get them looking identical. If you are doing two trees, simply divide the materials and work on them simultaneously. (The following quantities are for one tree only. Double them if you want to make a pair of trees.)

Note: The size of the dried Oasis or polystyrene sphere should correspond to the size of the pot. They will be in the right proportion if the sphere fits snugly when placed in the pot.

Materials

- Terracotta or stone planter pot
- Dried Oasis or polystyrene sphere (available from floristry supply stores)
- Dowel of appropriate length and thickness for size of sphere
- Filler (cement, plaster of Paris or one of the new expanding foam fillers available from hardware stores)
- Floristry wire
- Sharp scissors or wire-cutters
- Burgundy ribbon
- Dried flowers to suit your chosen colour scheme
- Walnuts or almonds (in their shells)
- Toothpicks
- Small Christmas ornaments, e.g. bells, cherubs, holly, pine-cones, etc.
- A large piece of polystyrene sheeting
- Gilding materials as on page 20

Method

1   Hold your piece of dowel in the centre of the pot, with the end of the dowel touching the floor of the pot. Now, remembering that the dowel must go right up into the middle of the sphere, cut to the appropriate length. Keeping the dowel in the exact centre of the planter pot, pour in the chosen filler, following the directions on the packet. I used an expanding foam filler because it is fairly light.

2   When the filler has dried, poke the toothpicks into the tiny holes in the bottom of each nut until the toothpick is firm and secure. Then poke the other ends of the toothpicks into the piece of polystyrene to facilitate the gilding of the nuts.

3   Gild each of the nuts (and any other decorations you wish to be gold), then gild the planter pot, the exposed filler and dowel, according to the directions on page 21.

4   When the gilding process is complete, centre the sphere over the dowel and push downward until the sphere feels securely attached to the dowel and looks nicely proportioned.

5   Cut the ribbon into lengths of about 6 cm. Loop them in half and gather the two ends together. Then wind a piece of floristry wire around the cut ends, securing them together. Leave a length of floristry wire unwound at the end. Make about fifteen of these ribbon loops and firmly poke them into the sphere at regular intervals.

6   If using dried flowers, poke small sprigs of these into the sphere, also at regular intervals. Follow with the gilded nuts on the toothpicks, pushing the toothpicks all the way into the sphere. Now add the rest of the objects. If they do not have anything on them that can be embedded into the sphere, either attach them to some floristry wire or glue a toothpick to the back of them.

7   Keep adding objects until the sphere is completely covered. Try to keep the objects at about the same level. For example, if a nut is protruding more than another ornament, pull the ornament out a little so that it becomes level with the nut.

8   For the finishing touch, tie a large bow and thread a piece of wire through the back of it. Using the wire, attach the bow to the underside of the sphere up where the dowel is embedded.

Christmas Wreath with Gilded Holly

A Christmas wreath on the front door extends good cheer to friends, family, neighbours and even passers-by. The addition of gilded holly leaves lends extra sparkle, whether it's a commercially-prepared wreath or one you have made yourself.

Here I have added gilded plastic holly leaves to a ready-made wreath. Dried holly leaves can also be gilded.

If you want to make your own wreath from scratch you'll need a dried Oasis circle (available from floristry supply stores) and similar objects to those used in the topiary tree in the previous project. Build these up in a similar fashion, making sure none of the base is visible. You'll end up with a very attractive and completely original wreath.

Pudding Halo

Whether using a pudding you have made yourself or one bought from the local store, you can make it look really special by the addition of some gilded plastic or dried holly. Place it evenly around your bowl or platter for a sumptuous effect.

Christmas Candle

A candle set in a gilded bowl adds a magical touch to any Christmas table setting. In this project, holly leaves were adhered to a wide-lipped bowl before gilding (see page 38).

Small pine-cones, pine-needles and burgundy ribbons have been arranged around the candle to add to the yuletide mood. The Balinese carved wooden angel has also been gilded, highlighting its interesting lines.

Opposite: *A Christmas tree aglow with gilded decorations and fairy lights brings a special sparkle to your home at Christmas time.*

Christmas Tree

The tradition of decorating trees to commemorate special days in the calendar can be traced back to ancient times — the Romans hung trinkets on trees during Saturnalia.

Queen Victoria's consort Prince Albert brought the German custom of bedecking fir trees with lighted candles at Christmas to England in the 1840s. These days, fairy lights have largely replaced candles — but the special magic of a beautifully decorated Christmas tree remains the focal point of our traditional yuletide celebrations.

Here I have gilded inexpensive plastic hearts and angels, transforming them into sumptuously glowing Christmas decorations that can be used year after year.

Gold-coloured Christmas balls and burgundy and gold bows offset the gilded decorations, and fairy lights highlight their warm sparkle.

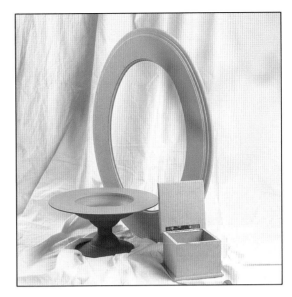

These raw craftwood objects, which were used in the projects in this book, are available from craft shops. The carved wooden frame was purchased from an importer of Indonesian furniture.

Upper left: *The raw craftwood box was used in the Document Box project on page36, and the little sliding drawer was used to make the Jewelled 'Book' on page 46.*

Lower left: *The small oval-shaped box, with an assortment of decorative mouldings, which was used to make the Bonbonniere pictured on page 55.*

Upper right: *The wide lipped bowl and oval mirror frame used in the Stiffened Fabric and Frame Bowl project on page 38.*

Lower right: *The raw wooden mirror frame which is photographed in its glided state on page 33.*

Gilding Kits

The attractively-packaged gilding kit pictured here is available from the author. It contains all the materials required for gilding, including:

- 25 sheets of Dutch gold leaf (15.5 cm x 15.5 cm)
- Gilding primer
- Gilding size
- Shellac flakes
- Antiquing finishes (black, white and Cafe Noir)
- Steelwool
- Pair of white cotton gloves
- 2 brushes
- Set of instructions

For those wishing to experiment on a smaller scale, a 'mini-kit' is also available. Products are in smaller quantities than those in the standard kit. The 'mini-kit' contains:

- 10 sheets of Dutch gold leaf
- Gilding primer
- Gilding size
- Shellac flakes
- Pair of white cotton gloves
- Set of instructions

All the products in each kit are available separately and in larger or smaller quantities, if required. Wholesale inquiries are welcome. For an information sheet, including prices (plus postage), write to Elisabeth Garratt at the following address:

> Elisabeth Garratt Interiors
> PO Box 7012
> St Kilda Road
> Melbourne VIC 3004

On receipt of payment, kits will be sent to any part of Australia or New Zealand.

Gilding Classes

The author gives gilding classes in the Melbourne metropolitan area. For inquiries, write to the above address.

Author's Acknowledgements

This book would not have been possible without the generous contributions made by the following:

Michael and Nadia Chernih of Gilded Ornaments, telephone (03) 9335 4336, for the donation of many of the exquisite mouldings and mirror and picture frames seen throughout this book, and also for their invaluable assistance in cheerfully supplying these items at a moment's notice; Jeannette Velisha of Botanica of Brighton, telephone (03) 9593 1729, for supplying the floral arrangements which adorn the pages of this book; Ivana Perkins of Handworks, telephone (03) 9820 8399; Sue Adair from the Craftree Folk and Decorative Art Workshop, telephone (03) 9596 3690; Joe D'Elia of Redelman; Yvonne Prince; Bernice Huggard; Cheryl Bradshaw and Robbyn MacDonald.

I would also like to express my gratitude to my family, with special thanks to :

Mr W. Andrew Thwaites for his immense kindness and warm-hearted generosity; the late Dr George Garratt for his benevolence and trust; my mother, Mrs Maria Maisano for placing her enviable bow-tying abilities, among other things, at my disposal; my sister Mrs Susanna McLean for sharing her eloquence and artistry, for being such a great support and my best friend; and my dear husband, Bruce, for his love, patience, understanding and unerring confidence in me and my abilities.

Pictorial Acknowledgements

The Publishers and the author express their gratitude to the National Gallery of Victoria, Melbourne, for permission to reproduce the following images:

Page 10

Egyptian c.320 BC–30 BC
Cartonnage mummy mask
Cartonnage, painted and gilded
56.0 x 40.6 cm
Felton Bequest, 1995

Page 11

Maitre Francois (French)
Wharncliffe Hours: Folio 7r
St John the Evangelist c.1475–80 (detail)
Illumination on vellum
17.8 x 12.5 cm
Felton Bequest, 1922

Page 13

Paolo Veneziano active 1320, died c.1358–62 (Italian)
The Crucifixion c.1349
Oil on wood
96.8 x 67.7 cm
Felton Bequest, 1949

They are also grateful to the late Justin O'Brien for permission to reproduce his painting on page 17. The details are as follows:

Justin O'Brien, 1917–1996 (Australian)
Madonna and Child, c.1950
Oil on board
107 **x** 84 cm
Private collection

Index

Glossary

Bole This soft clay containing iron oxide is traditionally applied under gold leaf. Often deep red in colour, it imparts a rich, warm hue to pure gold leaf, which is slightly transparent.

Burnished This means polished to a state of brilliance. This process can only be applied to pure gold leaf that has been water-gilded.

Dutch metal Another name for Dutch gold leaf, it is a composite of copper and zinc.

Gesso This mixture of fine chalk, called English whiting, and animal glue is used to fill in the grain of wood, providing the smooth, hard surface necessary for laying gold leaf. It must always be used for water-gilding but is not essential for Dutch gold leaf.

Gilding primer This contains a red oxide that simulates the red bole used in traditional gilding.

Ormolu Gilded bronze. Decorative objects made from bronze, including elegant clocks, were frequently overlaid with gold leaf, particularly during the rococo and Empire periods.

Shellac A resin made from the purified excreta of certain tropical insects. It is used in varnishes like French polish, and provides an ideal protective coating for Dutch gold leaf.

Shlagmetal Another term for Dutch gold leaf or Dutch metal.

Size This mixture of clay bole, distilled water and rabbit skin glue is an adhesive substance used to attach gold leaf.

Skewings Remnants of gold leaf. These can be re-used.

Variegated leaf These are leaves of copper to which heat has been applied, resulting in fiery reds, pinks, blues and greens blended with copper colour.